THE BASICS OF FOOD STORAGE

HOW TO BUILD AN EMERGENCY FOOD
STORAGE SUPPLY AS WELL AS TIPS TO STORE,
DRY, PACKAGE, AND FREEZE YOUR OWN
FOODS

DAVID NASH

PREFACE

Since you are reading a book on self-reliance, I am assuming you want to know more about how to take care of yourself in disaster situations

I would like to suggest you take a moment and visit my website and YouTube channel for thousands of hours of free content related to basic preparedness concepts

Dave's Homestead Website
https://www.tngun.com

Dave's Homestead YouTube Channel
https://www.youtube.com/tngun

Shepherd Publishing
https://www.shepherdpublish.com

HOW TO BUILD EMERGENCY FOOD STORAGE FOR ONLY $10 A WEEK

How to Build Emergency Food Storage for Only $10 A Week

As a preparedness advocate I have worked with many new preppers as they begin the preparedness journey. Many of them are so eager to make headway they they run headlong into debt trying to get prepared. That is not the way. Debt will only make the journey longer.

Rather than try to do everything at once, I would like to recommend just adding a little to each week's grocery shopping list. By going slower you can can go farther and with a lot less stress on your budget.

By spending $10 or $20 extra each week you can amass quite a stockpile of food almost without sacrifice.

Start at item one and each week purchase the next item on your list:

1. 6 Pounds of Salt
2. 5 Cans Cream of Chicken Soup
3. 20 Pounds of Sugar

4. 8 Cans Tomato Soup
5. 50 Pounds of Wheat
6. 6 Pounds of Macaroni
7. 20 Pounds of Sugar
8. 8 Cans of Tuna
9. 6 Pounds of Yeast
10. 50 Pounds of Wheat
11. 8 Cans of Tomato Soup
12. 20 Pounds of Sugar
13. 10 Pounds of Powdered Milk
14. 7 Boxes of Macaroni and Cheese
15. 50 Pounds of Wheat
16. 5 Cans of Cream of Chicken Soup
17. 1 Bottle of 500 Multi-Vitamins
18. 10 Pounds of Powdered Milk
19. 5 Cans of Cream of Mushroom Soup
20. 50 Pounds of Wheat
21. 8 Cans of Tomato Soup
22. Pounds of Sugar
23. 8 Cans of Tuna
24. 6 Pounds of Shortening
25. 50 Pounds of Wheat
26. 5 Pounds o f Honey
27. 10 Pounds of Powdered Milk
28. 20 Pounds of Sugar
29. 5 Pounds of Peanut Butter
30. 50 Pounds of Wheat
31. 7 Boxes of Macaroni and Cheese
32. 10 Pounds of Powdered Milk
33. 1 Bottle of 500 Aspirin
34. 5 cans of Cream of Chicken Soup
35. 50 Pounds of Wheat
36. 7 Boxes of Macaroni and Cheese
37. 6 Pounds of Salt
38. 20 Pounds of Sugar

39. 8 Cans of Tomato Soup
40. 50 Pounds of Wheat
41. 5 Cans of Cream of Chicken Soup
42. 20 Pounds of Sugar
43. 1 Bottle of 500 Multi-Vitamins
44. 8 Cans of Tuna
45. 50 Pounds of Wheat
46. 6 Pounds of Macaroni
47. 20 Pounds of Sugar
48. 5 Cans of Cream of Mushroom Soup
49. 5 Pounds of Honey
50. 20 Pounds of Sugar
51. 8 Cans of Tomato Soup
52. 50 Pounds of Wheat

There are some weeks in this process of food accumulation and storage when there will be money left over after your purchase.

Don't spend the money Instead, put it aside for use in the weeks when your purchase exceeds your budget. This will help you stick to the budget. In fact, there will also be weeks when the items you want to buy are on sale. Take full advantage of these sales to save money and get ahead.

Clearly, if you follow this shopping strategy, you will be able to meet your one year food storage goal while staying right at – or near – your pre-planned budget. This is something you can do, if you remain motivated and focused.

Now … for the really good news …

After a Year of the Plan, This is What You Would Have

You're about to be surprised, maybe even shocked, at what your 52-Week Food Storage Plan has enabled you to purchase and store for emergencies.

Within a year you will have accumulated all of the following:

- 500 Pounds of Wheat
- 100 Pounds of Sugar
- 40 Pounds of Powdered Milk
- 12 Pounds of Salt
- 10 Pounds of Honey
- 5 Pounds of Peanut Butter
- 45 Cans of Tomato Soup
- 15 Cans of Cream of Mushroom Soup
- 24 Cans of Tuna
- 15 Cans of Cream of Chicken Soup
- 21 Boxes of Macaroni and Cheese
- 500 Aspirin
- 1000 Multi-Vitamins
- 6 Pounds of Yeast
- 6 Pounds of Shortening
- 12 Pounds of Macaroni

Here is the BEST NEWS of all: the nutritional value for all of this food is, believe it or not, a whopping 1,249,329 calories (give or take a few calories). And, based on a daily diet in which you and your spouse each consume 2000 calories, the food listed above can sustain two people for about 312 days. That's the better part of a full year.

At a cost of just $10 per day – just $520 for a full year – this is a bargain you can't afford to pass up. In fact, it would still be a bargain if you doubled the cost because even if you were to spend $20 a week ... the cost to you would still be a modest $80 a month.

In 21st century America, you simply can't feed two people for such a small sum of money and remain healthy. Well, now you can. Put this amazing one year food storage plan to the test.

Start planning your first weekly purchase today.

TYPES OF FOOD STORAGE SYSTEMS AND OPTIONS

There are many philosophies and methods behind food storage systems and in my 3 decades as a prepper I have tried most all of them. Personal bias toward one system or another plays a large roll in selection, but so does budget, storage location, family disaster planning, and mindset. Rather than try simply persuade you to use the method I use, Let's take a few moments to describe common system pros and cons.

Prepackaged Commercial Freeze Dried Systems

It is possible to purchase packs of freeze dried foods conveniently prepackaged per meal or per person in units lasting from 72 hours to a full year. This is though to be the gold standard for preppers looking to stock a bug out location. For a person that has disposable income and does not desire to take the time to make an in depth plan, this is probably the best choice. However, it does have some drawbacks. First, this is the most expensive system. A year supply of quality food can easily cost 3-4 thousand dollars per person. However, that is not the only problem. You must look at the ingredients, as many plans that advertise "X" calories a day stuff their system with grain and other cheap means to inflate caloric counts. Others that advertise "servings" package ridiculously small portions.

Tip: Ignore any mention of "X" calories per person a day when calculating how much meal time you have stored, instead use a metabolic calculator (commonly found on diet websites) and input in your body type, activity level (think active for emergencies), height, and weight (or desired weight). The calculator will give you a caloric intake number for you. Use that number as your guide not the typical 2000 calorie a day generic recommendation.

Personally Packaged Bulk Foods

This is how I started building a food supply. I purchased 50 pound bags of wheat, beans, sugar, salt, and other staples and then packaged them using a variety of methods. Mostly using commercially available mylar bags and mason jars. Using oxygen absorber packets, you can get extremely long shelf life and a low per meal cost from building your own food storage system. In many of the following chapters you will find guidance for bulk packing your own long term food storage.

Many preppers get their start using a system based from the Church of Latter Day Saints, who have basic family preparedness as part of their beliefs. The Mormons have a food prep system based on having four main staples for an inexpensive and shelf stable system. The following amounts would keep a single person alive for a year.

- 5-12 pounds of Salt
- 35-100 pounds of Sugar (or honey)
- 30-50 pounds of Powdered milk
- 200-375 pounds of Hard Red Wheat, nitrogen-packed

The salt and sugar will last forever, although sugar packed with 02 absorbers will eventually become rock hard. The wheat will last for

30+ years if kept in an air tight container and away for heat and moisture. The Powdered milk, however, does have a relatively short shelf life. In all actually the dry milk you can purchase at the grocery is already close to, if not exceeded, its best by date. The fat in dry milk goes rancid quickly and it is best to buy this packaged in #10 cans and in no-fat versions. The local LDS storehouse used to allow non-members use their cannery equipment and buy form them in bulk, but things have changed. While not a member of the LDS church myself, I have often bought my milk and other staples from their website and from their canneries.

Just know that while stored whole wheat is cheap and lasts long enough to give to your heirs, it requires a grinder, and cheap grinders turn food preparation in to a long drawn our nightmare. Good grinders are expensive and the subject is long enough to deserve its own chapter later.

Tip: When storing food for your family know that plans are subject to change. A year supply for me, is only a 4 month supply now that I am I married and have a son. If my crazy sister, her worthless husband, and the three kids they still have living with them showed up at my house because they "knew I am a prepared for disasters," the 4 months of food security my family had dropped to just a little more than a month. Keep a little extra.

Meals Ready to Eat (MRE)

Before my time in the Marines, I had the idea that MREs were best for preppers and survivalists. After all, I reasoned, they are good enough for combat troops. However after several deployments I realized that they are heavy, bulky, and excessively packaged. As a civilian I also learned they are expensive, and have a short half life. My son likes them for the rush he gets playing soldier, but I grew out of that some years ago. I want something I can afford, that lasts a long times. MREs do not last very long if they are not stored in a cool location. However, they are convenient in the short term and are not a bad idea for short term operations, like a 72 hour kit or a bug out bag.

Store What You Eat, Eat What You Store

My farmer friends that are not "preppers" tend toward this model. It is good common sense to keep the things you eat on hand. By having a pantry stocked with items you use regularly you can be assured you always have a meal on hand and you can take advantage in sales.

During phases of the recent COVID-19 pandemic my local grocery store had a series of phases where certain foods became unavailable. That was inconvenient for my family to be sure, but it was not a crisis for us, as our pantry shelves acted like a grocery store, and the actual store was to restock our shelves. We keep 20 or so cans of things like soup, canned tomatoes, peas, and corn in our pantry and a can or two of each in the kitchen itself. We don't go to the store to get tonights supper, but rather to replenish our stock.

Tip: If you keep track of how much of a staple you use during the month (say toothpaste, toilet paper, or ketchup) and then multiple that by 12 you can see what you would need for a years supply.

Generic System

I use a mix of all because I want to reap all of the pros and reduce all the cons. I have a couple small 72 hour kits of freeze dried food for the weight savings in the event I have to leave my home in the night. I have a year or so of the LDS basics and have included other cheap and long storing staples like beans, and rice so I could cheaply and easily have a baseline storage level.

I don't have any MRE's currently, but if my 8 year old keeps his fascination with military life I will add a case or two.

The bulk of our system is a mixture of store-bought goods of canned goods, frozen meats, and shelf stable items like pasta. We round out the system by trying to produce a portion of our own meat and dairy on our farm, but I don't have the confidence to totally rely on my farming skill.

3

HOW TO MAKE YOUR FREEZER LAST WITHOUT ELECTRICITY

Because I have a couple of freezers full of food, I need to ensure they stay cold in the event a temporary disaster cuts power.

The first step is to cover the freezer with blankets to help retain the cold. Then, if possible add dry ice if it is available.

Since I moved to a more rural community dry ice is less available so I now keep several 2 liters of water frozen in my freezer for the same purpose. As an added benefit, shoehorning in water between food items makes the freezer more efficient.

When the power goes off I keep the door closed as much as possible, which makes the ice last longer.

Blanket coverings will keep a a full freezer frozen for two days, and the addition of ice (water or CO_2 based) will prolong that to 3 or 4 days.

If power stays off, it's time to eat and time to can the meat remaining.

Just remember, canning low acid foods such as meat requires a pressure canner, canning jars, and a source of consistent heat, and some skill.

4

HOW TO STORE FOOD WITH DRY ICE

Knowing how to store food with dry ice is an alternative to method to help preserve your food storage.

This method to use dry ice to store food is slightly more complicated than using Oxygen absorbers, but it is cheaper. Additionally, depending on your location, this method is easier to do. This is because most large grocery stores as well as welding supply companies have dry ice and most people have to order O2 absorbers online. You do want to make sure you are buying food grade dry ice since you will using this to store food.

Dry ice is just frozen carbon dioxide gas. A block of CO_2 warms to room temperature it turns into the harmless gas. One pound of the ice will turn into almost 8 and ½ cubic feet of gas. Therefore, it does not take much to fill the air spaces around your tiny grains of rice or wheat berries.

As a matter of fact, when using dry ice to replace the oxygen in your food storage buckets the biggest threat is that you use too much and pop the top of your bucket.

The big thing to remember when using dry ice to purge out and replace the air in you bucket is that quality matters. If you get dry ice that has water frozen inside it, water will be trapped at the bottom of your bucket... What you want to avoid is opening your wheat 30 years later to find the water has combined with your food to make nasty mold sludge instead of taste wheat goodness. You can tell you have water crystals in your dry ice because dry ice is light blue and frozen water is white. So when you are bringing your ice home keep it in a plastic container. Next, use a tight (but not airtight) lid. This is so that the constantly escaping CO_2 will push water away and let it form frost on your container and not your block.

How to Store Food With Dry Ice

Materials:

- Bucket with tight fitting lid
- Dry ice in plastic container (do not use glass or anything that will shatter if under pressure as you cannot get the Dry ice cold enough at your home to prevent it from turning back into gas)
- Hammer to break block
- Small scale – no need to be exact, but you need to be close
- Gloves (unless you want frost bite do not handle ice with bare skin)
- Food to be stored

Procedure:

1. Break your ice into small chunks (one ounce by weight will be about 1/6 cup by volume – approximately).
2. Pour one ounce (or two if you feel generous) into the bottom of your bucket and mound in a small pile in the center of your container.
3. Cover pile with a paper towel to keep your dry ice away from

your food (not strictly necessary, but it makes my wife feel better.

4. Fill bucket with food to ½ inch of headspace from top of bucket

5. Set the lid lightly on top and wait for ice to melt. If you seal lid the expanding gas will "explode" the bucket. Probably just popping the lid, but it could spew food throughout your house especially if your sealing powders like flour. You can seal the lid all the way around except for one small side.=

6. Feel the bottom of the bucket. If it is ice cold you still have solid CO_2. It should take 1 or so for the ice to dissipate.

7. As soon as the ice is turned to gas, seal the lid completely

8. Wait about 15 minutes and carefully check your buckets for signs of gas pressure. If the lids or sides of the bucket are bulged then you still had dry ice in the bucket and need to crack the seal carefully. Check again after 10 minutes.

9. After the bucket is sealed a vacuum may be present in your bucket and the sides may suck in a bit. This is normal and can be a good thing as no bugs will survive in a vacuum for long.

Yield:

5 pounds of ice (normally the minimum purchase) will do 40 buckets at 2 ounces per bucket.

Note:

This is not a project you can buy the materials and then do later. The ice will dissipate into CO_2 even if stored in your deep freeze. If you buy dry ice plan on using it within 5 or 6 hours.

HOW TO START POTTING MEAT

Potting Meat is a "if everything else fails" method. (Like the power is out long term and the blankets and ice isn't lasting long enough.)

This is an ancient food storage technique that worked for thousands of years.

Unfortunately, the USDA recommends against this process because of the potential for botulism.

Personally, I would rather pressure can meat. Canning is a much safer method, however crocking meat is still used as a culinary practice still used in France.

Potting (also known as crocking) meat is a process where meat is fully cooked and then placed in a sterile ceramic container and then covered with melted fat.

When the fat solidifies, the crock is covered and stored in a cool and dry location.

The idea is that the cooking destroys any bacteria in the meat and the fat covering seals the meat so that no new contamination can occur.

This is similar in mechanism to canning, except that the fat can insulate and botulism spores that were not destroyed – thereby locking them in the perfect conditions to grow.

Ingredients

- Meat (I used pork chops – which are perfect for crocking, but sausage, or bacon also work well)
- Fat (amount depends on the size of the crock and the amount of the meat, but I used a medium sized container of Manteca (pork fat).

Equipment:

- Skillet
- Pot
- Ceramic Crock
- Tongs

Procedure:

- Thoroughly clean a ceramic crock with very hot soapy water. *Items cannot be sterile until they are clean.*
- Sterilize by pouring boiling water into the crock. Hold the hot water in the crock until just before filling with meat.

- While water is boiling, melt some fat in a clean pot so you have enough grease to cover all the meat completely
- Completely cook meat until the internal temperature to be above 250°F.
- Empty the water from the crock and wipe the crock dry with a clean towel.
- Place hot grease in the bottom of the crock so that the bottom of the crock is covered.
- Place a layer of cooked meat into the crock.
- Cover with hot grease.
- Add another layer of meat and repeat adding hot grease.
- When the crock is full or you run out of meat, cover the meat with at least 2 to 3 inches of hot grease.
- Cover the crock with a plate or a cloth. Store the crock in a cool, dry place.
- When you want to eat your pork chops, remove the meat carefully. Place in a frying pan and re-fry and heat thoroughly. You want the internal temperature of the meat to reach at least 250°F again.

Yield:

Variable

Notes:

I believe that crocked meat is superior in flavor and taste to canned sausage patties or links, but with all things stored, you must trust your nose and other senses when cooking stored food. If anything seems off, discard the food.

6

HOW TO MAKE A MYLAR BAG CLAMP
FOR EASY BAG SEALING

As I get more involved with personal disaster preparation and I store more dry bulk foods, I keep looking for ways to make what I am doing simpler and easier while still being cost effective. One sure way of making your food storage program expensive is to allow waste. I absolutely hate throwing out food. Unfortunately, when I use an iron to try to seal a Mylar bag sometimes I don't get a good seal. If gone unnoticed this is a major source of waste.

A small needles sized hole will waste a perfectly good 02 absorber, while a large hole can (and has) spread sugar or beans all over your closet. Hopefully my DIY Mylar Bag Clamp will make it easier and faster to seal bags.

Searching for an Easier Way to Seal Mylar Bags

I have been searching for a solution to holding a full Mylar bag over the edge of a board while I try to juggle the bag, the iron, and the board while not dumping everything, burning myself, or taking to long with the seal so I won't exhaust the absorbers.

Commercial sealers are a clamp with a nichrome heating wire so they both hold and seal the bag. I have to compromise since I don't want to spend the cash to buy a commercial sealer so I am going to stay with the iron for sealing. That means I need a clamp.

Building a Sealing Clamp

While demolishing an old set of built in shelves I noticed one of the 2×4 boards had a mitered edge. I Thought to myself that this would be perfect to fold a bag edge around. I seal both 5 gallon and 1 gallon Mylar bags, so I cut two sections of 2×4 that were a little longer than the open end of a 5 gallon Mylar bag. Using a simple hinge from my scrap box I connected the two 2×4 sections together.

If I have a full bag, I can come over the top of the boards, and clamp the top of the bag between the boards. If I am going to make smaller bags, say for individual ration packs, I can put the entire empty bag in the clamp and fold the portion I am sealing over the top of the clamp.

How to Use This Homemade Clamp

By clamping the open ends of the boards together, it holds the bag, which makes it MUCH easier to iron. By facing the mitered edges of the board together, the "sharp" point also makes a crisp seal. I have noticed that when sealing using a board edge, its easy to get the bag crinkled, which does not seal very well.

Since I made the boards longer than needed, later I plan on drilling a small hole between the two boards, so that I can insert a vacuum sealer hose inside the bag so that I can partially evacuate the air before sealing so that I can use a smaller and less expensive 02 absorber.

This was a first attempt, and basically a proof of concept idea, but it works well, and since I only seal bags a couple times a year, I don't plan on building a tighter better constructed version unless the good idea fairy visits me again and I get a better idea.

SEAL MYLAR BAGS WITH A FOOD SEALER

There are many reasons to store bulk food. Bulk food is cheaper, and when you buy in bulk you insulate yourself from rising food costs. Bulk food storage is the backbone of long term emergency preparedness.

Anyone who has seen images of Haiti, or Katrina, or Tsunami survivors knows that our infrastructure is fragile. Even with the best efforts of government it takes time to get the wheels of commerce rolling again.

Bulk food storage using mylar bags is pretty simple. All you need to do is:

- Select the size of bag (1 or 5 gallon bags are most common) the thickness of the bag (I like bags that are between 4-7 mils in thickness).
- Fill with your selected food
- Add an oxygen absorber if needed (Sugar and Salt do not need O2 absorbers, and turn into bricks if used with one)
- Press shut and seal with an iron on medium heat.

The holy grail of food storage (at least for me) is to be able to seal mylar bags with a food sealer, but it is hard to get around the fact that no matter the brand, consumer vacuum sealers are not designed to work with mylar bags.

The inside of Mylar bags are smooth, whereas the insides of the plastic bags designed for use with vacuum sealers have ridges that allow air to freely flow out of the bag with the sides pressed together.

After much research into clamps, homemade vacuum chambers, and lots of trial and error it was discovered that a strip of corrugated plastic called coroplast can be used to create a channel that will allow the vacuum sealer to evacuate the air out of the bag.

Coroplast is most often associated with political yard signs, and is very easy to recycle.

Equipment:

- Mylar Bag (I prefer 7 mil one gallon bags)
- Foodsaver™ or other consumer vacuum sealer
- Strip of coroplast (approximately 1inch x 3 inch) – ensure the corrugated strips run lengthways.
- Mylar Impulse sealer or iron and small board as long as the bag is wide.

Procedure:

1. Fill your Mylar bag with food (or ammo or spare parts). Leave room for the sealer to
2. Insert the strip of coroplast into the bag, ensuring that one end is past the seals and into the vacuum chamber.
3. Activate the machine. In the model I have you press down on the lid until a light comes on indicating a good vacuum has been achieved.
4. The internal sealer is not strong enough to make a reliable seal with a thick Mylar bag. You will need to either use an impulse

sealer between the machine and the stored items in the bag, or you can place a board under the bag and seal it with an iron on medium heat.

Note:

Depending on your machine and the bags you use, you may need to experiment with the optimal placement of the coroplast strip. It took some fiddling until I could get a consistent seal.

HOW TO VACUUM SEAL FOOD WITHOUT A MACHINE

I like being able to vacuum seal my food storage, but I don't like having to rely on electricity to do it.

Trying to solve the problem of food storage without electricity led me to the earlier posts on my website Dave's Homestead to use mason jar adapter and a device called a Thrifty Vac. However, both of those posts use equipment.

You can remove air from a bag without any equipment and make an improvised vacuum seal.

My foodsaver does not work well with liquids. Obviously, no one wants to suck up any chicken juice into my machine. Normally I pack my bags, and then freeze them before I vacuum seal. However, I did not want to go through the hassle.

Also, I was also in the doghouse for too many kitchen messes and wanted to get done and get it cleaned before the wife came home...

Here is how I used ziplock bags to vacuum seal a bulk purchase of raw chicken without any special equipment

Equipment

- Ziplock bags
- Bowl (or just the plugged sink)
- Water (warm works better, but it does not matter)

Procedure

- Fill bag with item to be stored
- Partially close bag
- Immerse (but do not fully submerge) into the water – the weight of the water outside the bag is greater than the weight of the air inside the bag, so it will press in and force the air out of the bag. You may have to adjust the contents and press a little to get all the air out
- Once the air removed, close the bag and remove from the water.

If done correctly the bag will press against itself. If the two sides of the bag are not pressed tightly together you did not remove all the air.

FREEZING ORANGES FOR LONG TERM STORAGE

Freezing oranges is the easiest thing in the world to do. The question is why freeze oranges. I do it because we like to buy in bulk in season, and this allows me to keep some around all year long.

I also find that frozen oranges juice better. Additionally, I have a personal habit of chewing on a frozen slice of orange when I come in from the heat of mowing the yard or other activity. I have also found it to be useful for teething babies if you use a smaller and sweeter orange that is not very tart.

To Freeze Oranges:

- Simply peel them and break them into segments.
- Arrange the orange segments on a cookie sheet in a single layer.
- Pack them as tight as you want, but it is best if the oranges don't touch. Items that are touching when they are frozen tend to stick together.
- Freeze.

Once frozen you can back in bulk and they orange segments won't stick together. This process works with other items. I do it for make ahead burritos and blackberries all the time.

We did this with bananas and used the frozen fruits to make a non-dairy ice cream.

LONG-TERM WATER STORAGE

As a prepper, it's easy to get tunnel vision, storing food, learning skills, acquiring gear. I find a tendency to forget about the most basic needs because they are always there in the background.

Do Not Overlook the Importance of Clean Water

The most overlooked resource is water. For pure survival water is second only to oxygen. We can only last a few hours to a few days without water. Few people store it in any quantity.

I know water is heavy. It can leak. It can be a pain. However, you must have some water storage as well as means to purify it once your store runs low. One of our first videos was on a simple bucket filter made out of a ceramic filter and some food grade buckets. And that filter has gone on to become a commercial success and is widely available four around $20.00, but where are you going to get the water from to fill it?

Find Water Sources Now!

Go out now and find sources of water in your area, but remember, this is a base need, and a small creek in the back of the subdivision may not supply enough water for EVERYONE in the subdivision that knows about it.

FEMA and the Red Cross have long suggested storing 1 gallon per person in your household per day for three days, but that is not enough. That small amount is going to be used up quickly in just drinking and cooking. Have you ever tried to clean yourself with less than a gallon of water?

I am just barely prepared in this area, as I only have a 5 gallon jerry can per day for my wife and me. It is on "my list" to prepare a rain water barrel, and to store a 55 gallon drum of potable water in my basement, but to be honest, "cooler" projects seem to always win out when I am planning my next project.

On my website, Dave's Homestead I show you how to make liquid bleach and a simple chlorine generator for water purification, but let's start simple.

Store Enough Water

Today we are just going to go over how to store a base amount of water in your house to fulfill the ready.gov ideal of 72 hours.

The first thing you're going to need is something to store your water in. I use 5 gallon jerry cans (they are less than $10 each, sturdy, and have a handle). But they can be heavy and awkward to use. Many people I know use 2 liter soda bottles since they are a lot easier to carry, even if they are not as sturdy. Do not become tempted and try to use milk jugs, as it is impossible to clean out the milk residue and it becomes a breeding ground for bacteria. Whatever you use, it needs to be food grade, clean, and able to be closed.

Fill you container with clean water, the purer the better. Add bleach. I follow the FEMA guidelines of 1 teaspoon of non-scented bleach per gallon of water. The bleach and water mix should smell slightly of chlorine. It's safe, since the chlorine looses its effective-ness over time and will eventually degrade. When filling and capping, make sure your don't recontaminate the container with your hands.

Store your water in a cool dry place, out of direct sunlight to protect the plastic.

This water does have a shelf-life, so twice a year, when I set the clock for daylight savings, and after I change the smoke detector batteries, I dump the water and refill the containers.

HOW TO PURIFY WATER USING POOL SHOCK

2 is one and one is none. I need another means of water purification other than my ceramic water filter. I wanted something that stored indefinitely, was cheap, and most importantly kills all the bad junk in the water.

There are many preparedness blogs that discuss using hypochlorite to make bleach. This one I wade through the differences between sodium and calcium hypochlorites. I also give dosing amounts.

I found the sources below and decided on this method of using Pool Shock for Water Purification

Many campers use bleach for water purification. However, bleach degrades over time. It only has an effective shelf life of 6 months to a year.

Dry High Test Hypochlorite (HTH) has no shelf life, and its cheap. A one pound bag (that will purify about 10,000 gallons of water) is about $5.00.

I spent a little more ($24.00) and bought a five pound jug (which is a LIFETIME) supply because it can be resealed.

I will tell you though that this is not a perfect solution, this stuff is a powerful corrosive and if you don't store this properly you WILL have problems.

• If it gets wet it can off-gas chlorine.

• It can corrode metals

• If certain petroleum products mix with the HTH it can spontaneously ignite in a way you do NOT want to see.

Granular Calcium Hypochlorite

Only use HTH Pool Shock that does not have any algicides or fungicides. Ingredients should reads CALCIUM hypochlorite and inert ingredients. Use a brand with at least 73% Hypochlorite.

For this video I used Poolife Turboshock, but feel free to use any brand you wish as long as it fits the perimeters above.

Before you begin mixing any chemicals in any way, please follow basic safety precautions. Make sure you do this in a ventilated area. Have plenty of water to dilute any mistakes. Wear eye protection for splashes. Lastly always mix the powder into the water NOT the other way around.

Add and dissolve one heaping teaspoon of high-test granular calcium hypochlorite (HTH) (approximately 1/4 ounce) for each two gallons of water.

The mixture will produce a chlorine solution of approximately 500 mg/L (0.0667632356 oz per US gallon), since the calcium hypochlorite has an available chlorine equal to 70 percent of its weight.

To disinfect water, add the chlorine solution in the ratio of one part of chlorine solution to each 100 parts of water to be treated. This is roughly equal to adding 1 pint (16 oz.) of stock chlorine to each 12.5 gallons of water to be disinfected.

To remove any objectionable chlorine odor, aerate the water by pouring it back and forth into containers to add air.

Chlorine Bleach

Common household bleach (unscented) contains a chlorine compound that will disinfect water. The procedure to be followed is usually written on the label. When the necessary procedure is not given, find the percentage of available chlorine on the label and use the information in the following tabulation as a guide.

Available Chlorine Drops per Quart of Clear Water

• 1% needs 10 Drops

• 4-6% needs 2 Drops

• 7-10% needs 1 Drops

(If strength is unknown, add ten drops per quart of water. Double amount of chlorine for cloudy or colored water)

The treated water should be mixed thoroughly and allowed to stand for 30 minutes. The water should have a slight chlorine odor; if not, repeat the dosage and allow the water to stand for an additional 15 minutes.

FEMA and the Red Cross have guidelines on how much clorine to put in water for drinking, this makes the chlorine not the purified water. DO NOT DRINK THIS MIX. Put it in the water you will drink.

WHEAT GRINDING BASICS: TYPES OF WHEAT GRINDERS

If you're going to store wheat, you need to be able to grind it. And while it has been ground in the past by throwing some in a metal coffee can and hammering a piece of iron pipe into the grain until its broken up, that way is loud, long, and energy intensive. In my book 52 Unique Techniques for Stocking Food for Preppers I actually show the iron pipe method.

It's a lot simpler to buy a wheat grinder. However, there is a huge difference in price and many types of wheat grinders. Below are some of the basic differences as a starting point for you to be able to decide what type is best for your intended use.

There are three basic types of grinders:

Stone

The oldest grinder are stone wheels. Until recently they were the only type available. Stone grinders have two circular stones. One stone is stationary, and the second turns against it. Starting at the center of the stone and radiating outward, grooves are cut into the stone. These grooves become shallower as they near the ends of the stone, until they disappear at the outer edges. When grain is ground, it falls through a channel into the center of the two stones. As the stone rotates, it pulls the grain out through the channels where it is ground. As the grain rides in the channel it becomes ground progressively finer until flour falls out the outer edges of the two stones.

Historically, stones in grist mills were three feet or more across, and weighed hundreds of pounds. This took the force of a water wheel, or windmill to turn. Modern stones are much smaller, now only inches, and are not made from natural stone, but now use either cast iron or artificial stone.

Stone grinders are very durable and will last a lifetime if not abused.

Favorable Characteristics

• Very durable

• Adjustable to any setting from cracked wheat to fine flour

• Less likely to be damaged from foreign particles such as pebbles sometimes found in bulk grain.

• Should last a lifetime

Unfavorable Characteristics

• Usually larger, bulky machines that can't easily stored

• Grind more slowly than impact grinders

• Stones quickly become `loaded' if you grind oil bearing seeds or nuts

Burr

Burr grinders are nearly identical to stone grinders except their grinding wheels are made out of steel with small teeth protruding out the sides. These teeth shear the grain into flour. Burr grinders have some advantages and disadvantages over stone grinders.

Favorable Characteristics

• Will grind dry grains as well as oil bearing seeds (wheels will not "load up".)

Unfavorable Characteristics

• Will not grind as finely as a stone grinder.

Impact

Impact grinders use rows of 'blades' placed in circular rows on metal wheels. Like a stone grinder, one wheel turns and the other wheel is stationary. The two wheels are aligned so that the rows of blades inter-mesh. As the wheel turns at thousands of RPM, the closely aligned blades pulverize the grain into fine flour as the grain works its way to the outside of the wheels.

Favorable Characteristics

• Very small, light and compact.

• Grinds very quickly

• Grinds grain into very fine flour

Unfavorable Characteristics

• Small rocks or metal pieces will damage and cause a misalignment of the wheels.

• Noisy

• Even on the coarsest setting the flour comes out fine. (You won't be able to crack wheat.)

• Electric only, you cannot get a manual impact grinder.

Manual or Electric

Once again, this depends on your use. You need a manual grinder if your need if for your disaster food storage, but you need to be aware that it is more work than you would think to grind wheat, especially with an inexpensive grinder. I would suggest that if you buy a manual grinder (and you should have one) that it has a pulley along with a crank, so you can mechanize it if needed. There are internet plans to hook a grinder to a stationary bike.

Electric make short work of grain grinding, but with impact mill the trade off is that a quite impact mill sounds like a vacuum cleaner, and a loud one will positively hurt your ears. Also you need to be aware that some electric powered mills grind so fast that they create enough heat to harm your flour. Your wheat will taste better if ground slow so that the mill stays cool. Electric mills are also the most expensive option, but you will find it worth it if you begin to use your mill to grind flour now, and get used to fresh bread before you are forced to eat out of your store.

You know I like redundancy, and I would suggest getting both. Personally, since the mill I want costs as much as the Glock I want to buy my wife, it's on "the list" but I do have two manual mills so I have one for a spare or to trade.

13

HOW TO MAKE HARDTACK: EVERY PREPPER'S FIRST FOOD STORAGE RECIPE

What is Hardtack?

Hardtack is basically a large hard cracker that was a staple of the civil war soldier's diet, however, while it was best known for its role in that conflict, hardtack had been used long before that war, and for feeding other groups such as sailors and outdoors-men. Hardtack Crackers seem to be a prepper rite of passage, it seems like all preppers try their hand at making them. I believe it is because of the ease of manufacture, low cost, and high storage stability. It sure isn't for the taste.

Hardtack has been used in various forms and using various grains as a base since the time of the Egyptian pharaohs, and it is still made today by a factory in Virginia for use in Alaska. Anyone that needs a shelf stable, long lasting light weight food should consider hardtack.

The secret to its success is that it has no fat to go rancid, and no moisture to cause it to spoil. The only ingredients are flour, salt, and water to form the dough. It is then rolled into 1/8 to ½ inch sheets and baked until the moisture is driven out.

Traditional Ways to Eat Hardtack

The problem with hardtack is that it is, well, hard. This hardness helps it travel well, but makes it hard to eat. Normally hardtack is crumbled into a soup or coffee and eaten as a mush, or it is soaked in brine and cooked, or cooked with meats in a skillet. Very seldom is it actually eaten as a whole unbroken cracker. This probably is why it was "affectionately" named teeth-breakers by some soldiers.

It's simple to make, and as a side note, its pretty much the base of most dog biscuits (Or occasional Rabbit treats)

My Favorite way to Eat Hardtack

If I am going to eat a hard biscuit, I like to soak it in water or milk for about 15 minutes, and then fry in a buttered skillet.

This goes well with cheese, soup, or just plain with a salt.

How to Make Hardtack

Ingredients:

- 6 cup flour
- 1 cup water
- 1 tablespoon salt

Procedure:

1. Knead dough until thoroughly mixed.
2. Roll out on a floured surface until about 1/8 inch thick (or thicker if desired).
3. Cut into biscuits – traditionally it was square, but I like mine round.
4. Use a fort to poke holes in the hardtack; this is not for looks,

but to allow steam to escape while cooking and to ensure complete cooking.

5. Bake at 325 for at least an hour, turning over the hard tack once. Check to see that it is cooked through completely. Take out & let cool overnight to get that real hard & dry feeling.

   Hardtack for naval use was traditionally baked another 3 times to ensure there was no moisture left.

A basic hardtack should keep for years as long as it is kept in an airtight container.

14

MAKING WHEAT BERRY PANCAKES IN A BLENDER

Of all the food storage recipes I make, wheat berry blender pancakes is my wife's favorite. Its also a winner on a weekend morning, because its easy, cheap, and gets me points for when I plan on spending the day on a project that Genny doesn't want to help me with...

If you really want a healthy treat, use buttermilk and let the wheat berries soak in it overnight. The acid in the milk helps break up the wheat making it more digestible (it also makes it taste better).

This is a very healthy recipe that does not sacrifice taste. One thing I must note is that wheat berry blender pancakes need to be blended very well or you can get bits of whole wheat in your pancake. Be patient with the blender, and soaking overnight in buttermilk is well worth it, but this is a super simple recipe, and if you get an urge for pancakes you can just throw it all in the blender for a really quick meal.

Making Wheat Berry Pancakes in a Blender:

Ingredients:

• 1 Cup Milk (translation for powdered milk is 3 T. Milk and 1 C. Water)

- 1 Cup Wheat Berries

- 2 Eggs (2 T. powdered eggs 1/4 C. Water)

- 2 tsp Baking Powder

- 1-1/2 tsp Salt

- 2 Tbs. Oil

- 2 Tbs. Honey or Sugar

Procedure:

1. Add the wheat and milk in the blender and pulse until the wheat turns to batter.

2. Add the other ingredients and pulse for a couple minutes more.

This works because the blender is made to mix wet ingredients and so it works best with liquids. After every couple pancakes pulse the batter for a second of two to keep everything mixed.

If you do not eat a lot of whole wheat, but keep some for food storage know that changing your diet from the typical modern foodstuffs to a diet based on whole grain will cause a painful readjustment period. I find recipes like this and the ones found in Book 6 of the Homestead Series (Basic Baking) makes it easy to keep whole grains on the menu enough to keeps your pipes plumbed for whole grain.

15

DEHYDRATING GARLIC

I love garlic, both for cooking, and for medicine. But mostly I love dry garlic for cooking. I put garlic powder in almost everything.

Unfortunately, garlic powder is getting more expensive, which is silly because of how easy it is to dehydrate garlic.

To make my own garlic powder I simply grind dehydrated garlic and then sift it.

The large chunks go in an old minced garlic container, while the finer bits go in the reused garlic powder container.

To dehydrate it simply:

- Peel back the paper from the cloves of garlic.
- Cut out any bad spots with a knife.
- Cut the cloves in half lengthwise to significantly reduce the time it will take to dry.
- Dry the garlic at 150 degrees Fahrenheit (in the oven or in a dehydrator)
- Turn the slice often until dry.

- Once you have it ground and put into your container, store in a cool, dry area.

I don't know how long it lasts, as I continuously use it, so I don't have information on powdered garlic for food storage.

What I do know is that I like the taste of the garlic I grew and processed myself. There is something to be said about the quality of food that is home processed versus being made in some factory out of materials that may be modified or adulterated.

Not only is dehydrating garlic easy, but garlic has medicinal value, so I hope that you try this at home.

16

HOW TO MAKE SUN DRIED TOMATOES

Seasoned Sun Dried Tomatoes packed in good olive oil is a great addition to your food storage system.

They taste great in salads and other dishes, as well as giving some variety from tomato sauce, salsa, and paste.

This is a simple recipe and if you can grow tomatoes, you can make this recipe.

How to Make Sun Dried Tomatoes

Ingredients:

- Tomatoes
- Any quantity, ripe, but not over ripe. Yield varies depending upon the moisture content of the tomatoes. Paste tomatoes (Roma) work best and typically yield 2 cups of dried tomatoes for each 5 lbs of fresh.
- Olive oil
- Spices (garlic, basil, salt)

Equipment:

one of the following:

- Oven OR
- Food dehydrator OR
- Car on a hot sunny day

Procedure:

- Fist, slice the tomatoes
- If you desire season the tomatoes with sea salt, kosher salt and/or some spices (typically basil).
- Next, dry them using one of several methods
- Then, when done, the tomatoes should be flexible, like a raisin from a fresh bag; not brittle. Most describe them as leathery with a deep red color, without free water or a tacky feeling. The first time I did this, I dried them too much and they did not absorb the oil very well.
- Finally, fill a mason jar with the slices and top to 1 inch of head space with oil. (I also like to throw in a little basin and garlic in the jar)

Drying Methods

Drying with a Food dehydrator:

- Arrange the pieces on each rack so that air can circulate, preferably with the pieces not touching each other, but there's no need to become obsessive about it. Turn the dehydrator on and enjoy the aroma. If your food drier has a thermostat, set it for 140 degrees F. It will take 3 to 8 hours.

Drying in an Oven:

- preheat the oven to 150 degrees F (65 degrees C or gas mark 1). If you don't have these settings, just use the lowest setting you've got. Arrange the tomatoes on cake racks, spread out, not touching each other. Cookie sheets will work if you don't have cake racks or screens – but you need to flip or stir the tomatoes once in a while to expose the other side of them.. Close the oven. It takes about 10 to 20 hours, but you'll need to check periodically, including rotating the shelves and moving them up or down to get even heating.

Drying Using an Automobile and a hot sunny day:

- Spread the tomato slices out on shallow trays. Cover them loosely with cheesecloth to keep any potential for bugs to come in contact. Put the trays on the dashboard of your car and roll all the windows up and park in the sunniest spot you've got. It's best to start in the morning and let it go to sunset. It may take 2 days – bring the tomatoes in the house overnight.

17

USING AN EXCALIBUR TO DEHYDRATE FRUIT

I am used to the round Nesco dehydrators; I own several and have used them for decades. However, I have always wanted an Excalibur Dehydrator, I just hesitated at spending the money but a good friend of mine let me use his to see if it was worth the expense.

In my opinion, and the opinion of several other reviewers, a dehydrator is a dehydrator, is a dehydrator when it comes to the amount of time it takes to work.

Strawberries that take 6 hours to dry in my round Nesco, take the same 6 hours in the larger Excalibur.

The difference comes in the EASE of use.

The rectangular Excalibur trays allow me to more easily fit items in the tray, and when making things like jerky, or spreadables like bean bark or fruit roll up, it is much easier to fit thinks on a square tray than a round one with a hole in the center.

Something else I really liked was the double tray; you have a plastic tray with a very large grate that holds a removable flexible mesh that your food sits on. This allows you to pick up the whole mesh tray by the corners and use it like a funnel to pour your dehydrated foods into their containers. With the round Nesco It seems like I keep dropping the food off the tray as I try to box the food up.

The Excaliber is much more flexible than the round dehydrators. You can even take the trays out and use it as an incubator for bread dough or yogurt.

Depending on who you are and what your circumstances are, the size may be a positive or a negative. I like how big it is, because I do my food storage in bursts – I do a lot at a time, and I don't like to wait on one batch to finish so I can start another. However, space is a premium in my home, so I don't have a dedicated place to keep it out – so I will wait until we get the homestead built and I have a dedicated food prep room before I get my own.

I think this dehydrator is worth the price – even if it does cost a couple hundred dollars.

So that was the review – now let's talk about ways to keep fruit from browning while dehydrating

You Can Use:

- Steam for 3-4 minutes: You need to rinse with cold water and blot dry before dehydrating.
- Lemon, lime, pineapple juice and water: 1:4 -one quart water to one cup juice
- Citric Acid: Mix 1 teaspoon of citric acid into one of cold water. Let soak for 10 minutes
- Ascorbic acid: Stir 2 1/2 tablespoons of pure ascorbic acid crystals into one quart of cold water. (6 500 milligram vitamin c tablets = 1 teaspoon ascorbic acid) Soak for 10 minutes.
- Honey Dip: Mix ½ cup sugar with 1½ cups boiling water. Cool to lukewarm and add ½ cup honey Place fruit in dip and soak 3 to 5 minutes.

All of these help control oxidation that causes browning. I like the lemon juice the best because it is easy and cheap, but the honey dip tastes better.

PLEASE REVIEW

Please visit my Amazon Author Page at:

https://amazon.com/author/davidnash

if you like my work, you can really help me by publishing a review on Amazon.

The link to review this work at Amazon is:

https://www.amazon.com/review/create-review?asin=B07YGP4P2R

LINKS TO VIDEOS

The Basics of Food Storage: Playlist

http://yt.vu/p/PLZH3jGjLQ0rBliKZ7cBCkfd2cLPLmLXvH

How to Make Your Freezer Last Without Electricity

https://youtu.be/lAH7Lp5hOug

How to Store Food With Dry Ice

https://youtu.be/vtJ8PkyYbog

How to Make a Mylar Bag Clamp for Easy Bag Sealing

https://youtu.be/XQd3QRylFYk

How to Use Mylar Bags for Bulk Food Storage

https://youtu.be/m_V-DZdfwjQ

How To Freeze Oranges for Long Term Storage

https://youtu.be/sCvtLD-wJSc

How to Make Hardtack

https://youtu.be/tql6Z9Z-MEQ

How to Vacuum Seal Food Without a Machine

https://youtu.be/9Lh6lGj20Jw

How to Bulk Store Hamburger

https://youtu.be/eCevmhbb4yU

How to Make Brandied Strawberries

https://youtu.be/REo_sYpUf3I

How to Freeze Peppers

https://youtu.be/_oyRynIWRsA

How to Store Water Long-Term

https://youtu.be/iAQPhe08Cvg

How to Purify Water Using Pool Shock

https://youtu.be/o6e0_tZWTuc

How to Grind Wheat Using a Cheap Hand Mill

https://youtu.be/jW1htxghQYs

How to Make Wheat Berry Pancakes in a Blender

https://youtu.be/9jPjk-LIK7I

How to Make Sun Dried Tomatoes

https://youtu.be/5k4QFqBWjHQ

How to Use an Excalibur to Dehydrate Fruit

https://youtu.be/CgG6YNCstv4

BONUS: EXCERPT FROM 21 DAYS TO BASIC PREPAREDNESS

There are quite a few schools of thought when it comes to personal disaster preparedness. The largest seems to be concerned with "Stuff". I call this the government model. In this model, practitioners buy gear to solve problems. They seem to feel that money equals solutions.

While you do need to have some level of resources, I feel this is a mistake, because stuff can get stolen, damaged, or lost. If you rely solely on gear, then no matter how redundant you think you are, you still have a single point of failure.

I believe in a balanced approach. In this document, I will illustrate basic concepts for disaster preparedness as well as give you some solid tips and steps to help you begin to prepare.

There is very little in the way of gear acquisition written in the following pages. You will need to acquire some measure of food, water, and equipment if you are to become more disaster resilient, however, there are multitudes of resources on and off line to help you do just that.

What is this book is designed to do is to guide you through the first steps of personal preparedness, i.e., "getting your mind right". I find that without a solid set of guideposts, it is easy to fall down the rabbit hole and concentrate only on buying stuff, or gaining training. Both of which are necessary, but neither will allow you the flexibility to adapt, improvise, or overcome.

Venn diagram of the relationship between skills, stuff, and training

I want you to be balanced, to have the right mix of things *and* skills with a strong mindset to be able to thrive in any situation.

I do not have all the answers, but I have spent decade's figuring out the best solutions for my family. Everything I wrote here are things I have done, and it has worked well for me. Take it as a guide and a starting point, question everything, and find your own solutions.

I have taken the liberty of writing this as if we were sitting in your living room talking; it is informal because preparedness does not have to be stressful.

Please do not mistake my familiar terms for ignorance of the subject. I have a degree in Emergency Management, hold certification as Emergency Management Professional, and have over a decade in planning and teaching Emergency Management in state service as well as a lifetime of doing this with my family.

If you like this Introduction to 21 Days to Basic Preparedness, you can find it on Amazon.

ALSO BY DAVID NASH

Fiction

The Deserter: Legion Chronicles Book 1

The Revolution: Legion Chronicles Book 2

The Return: Legion Chronicles Book 3

The Warrior: Legion Chronicles Book 4

Homestead Basics

The Basics of Raising Backyard Chickens

The Basics of Raising Backyard Rabbits

The Basics of Beginning Beekeeping

The Basics of Making Homemade Cheese

The Basics of Making Homemade Wine and Vinegar

The Basics of Making Homemade Cleaning Supplies

The Basics of Baking

The Basics of Food Preservation

The Basics of Food Storage

The Basics of Cooking Meat

The Basics of Make Ahead Mixes

The Basics of Beginning Leatherwork

Non Fiction

21 Days to Basic Preparedness

52 Prepper Projects

52 Prepper Projects for Parents and Kids

52 Unique Techniques for Stocking Food for Preppers

Basic Survival: A Beginner's Guide

Building a Get Home Bag

Handguns for Self Defense

How I Built a Ferrocement "Boulder Bunker"

New Instructor Survival Guide

The Prepper's Guide to Foraging

The Prepper's Guide to Foraging: Revised 2nd Edition

The Ultimate Guide to Pepper Spray

Understanding the Use of Handguns for Self Defense

Note and Record Books

Correction Officer's Notebook

Get Healthy Notebook

Rabbitry Records

Collections and Box Sets

Preparedness Collection

Legion Chronicles Trilogy

Homestead Basics: Books 1-6

Translations

La Guía Definitiva Para El Spray De Pimienta

Multimedia

Alternative Energy

Firearm Manuals

Military Manuals 2 Disk Set

ABOUT THE AUTHOR

 David Nash is a homesteader with chickens, bees, rabbits, goats, and a couple of pigs. For a while he even had an extensive aquaponics setup in his basement, until his long-suffering wife made him eat all the fish.

He knows how to raise animals humanely, simply, and without angering the neighbors. Dave runs a popular YouTube channel on DIY homesteading as well as being the author of several books on DIY preparedness and urban homesteading topics.

In fact, the tips shown in this book contributed to him receiving the third highest preparedness score on the TV show Doomsday Preppers

He is a father and a husband. He enjoys time with his young son William Tell and his school teacher wife Genny. When not working, writing, creating content for YouTube, playing on his self-reliance blog, or smoking award-winning BBQ he is asleep or on his tractor - but not both at the same time.

amazon.com/author/davidnash

facebook.com/booksbynash

youtube.com//tngun

goodreads.com/david_allen_nash

twitter.com/dnash1974

instagram.com/shepherdschool

pinterest.com/tngun

Contents

Introduction v

Model Prayer Review 1

Lead Us 11

Deliver Us 41

Introduction

PRAYER IS POWERFUL.

It connects us to God.

It makes tremendous power available to us.

Prayer allows us to escape the pressures of this world and enter the heavenly realm.

Prayer also allows us to bring the powers of the heavenlies down to earth.

There has never been a great move of God without prayer.

So, doesn't it stand to reason that we should all learn how to pray?

Fortunately, Christ gave us a map on how to pray, which many people call the Lord's Prayer. This model prayer enables us to pray more effectively as believers. This is book four of five, in which we will dive into two of the most essential topics for every believer to understand in order to pray more accurately and effectively.

Protection and Guidance

We all need daily protection and guidance. The difference between life and death is found in our ability to receive these from our Father. Whether we will accomplish our destiny or fumble our way through life is determined by how we handle these two essential components of the Christian walk. We need daily help, but thankfully, we have a God who provides daily guidance and protection, making it readily available to us. So, how do we access it? Christ laid out the answer for us in the Model Prayer. Let's read on and receive our daily help!

Model Prayer Review

Model Prayer Review

EACH BOOK GOES THROUGH WHAT IS commonly referred to as the Lord's Prayer. We have determined in book one of this series that this is really a misnomer, because forgiveness is asked for in the prayer and we know that Jesus never sinned. Therefore, He had no reason to ask for forgiveness. Jesus was actually giving us an example, an outline, a model for us to pattern our own prayers after. The Lord's Prayer could be more accurately referred to as the Model Prayer. Within the framework of this outline, there are several headings. For example, we have covered:

- *"Our Father" (heading number 1)*
- *"Who art in heaven" (heading number 2)*

- *"Hallowed be Thy name" (heading number 3)*

The headings comprising the prayer were never meant to just be prayed word for word. The headings are the structure of the outline, which gives you a formula for how you ought to shape your prayers, so when you say, "Our Father, who art in heaven, hallowed be Thy name," you have just uttered a list of headings. But based on your knowledge of the Scriptures, based on your relationship with God, based on your individual situations, and based upon your particular needs at the time, you will determine how you fill in the gaps after every heading.

This model prayer is an outline, and as such, an outline can be expanded or condensed as much or as little as you wish. In other words, this model can be used for a three- to five-minute prayer, or it can be used for a ten- to fifteen-minute prayer. The same model can be used for a thirty-minute prayer, a forty-five-minute prayer, or a fifty-minute prayer, and it's the same model those of us who know about tarrying before God use for our longer prayers. The same model can be used for hourlong, two-hour, or three-hour prayers.

However long you decide to pray or feel led to pray, when you follow this model, you will cover every area of your life.

Between the moment you said "Our Father" and the moment you say "Amen," there will not be any need or issue in your life that you will not have touched.

The structure in this prayer model has a flow to it, and you are urged to go with that flow. The headings in the outline are divided into three major categories. Category number one is all about God:

- Our *Father*, hallowed be *Thy* name. *Thy* kingdom come. *Thy* will be done.

Category two is all about us:

- Give *us* this day *our* daily bread. Lead *us* not into temptation. Deliver *us* from evil.

3

LEAD US & DELIVER US

Category three takes us back to God:

- For *Thine* is the kingdom, and the power, and the glory forever and ever. Amen.

The prayer begins with God and the prayer ends with God. Some theologians regard this as a "sandwich structure"—God on the two ends, with us in the middle.

In book number one, we discovered what the first three headings are all about. For the first heading—"Our Father"—we learned we are not an only child; we have siblings, and we have a loving Father. Under the second heading, we remember His position over us, that His ways and His thoughts are far above ours, and that He has a perfect vantage point to see what is coming down the road for us. So, even when circumstances catch us by surprise, they are no surprise to God. Under the third heading, we are told to give honor and glory to God's name. We considered many of the names for God listed in His Word and how those names give us insight into His nature.

In book number two, we considered the headings: "Thy kingdom come" and "Thy will be done, on earth as it is in heaven." Under the heading "Thy kingdom come," we learned that God will not force His kingdom upon you, nor will He withhold it from you. At any point in time, should you choose to come to Him or return to Him after a time spent away, He will accept you with open arms. It is His pleasure to welcome His children into the family and the royal priesthood that He has prepared for them. We learned that a kingdom is simply two words put together: *king's domain*. Essentially, when we pray for God's kingdom to come, we are praying for His rule and His reign to come into our lives. When the Lord reigns, peace reigns, joy is evidenced, and purpose, clarity, and wisdom are freely given. There is no shortage of His supply or support. We also considered the heading "Thy will be done on earth as it is in heaven." We discovered the differences between the decreed, or the sovereign will of God, the perceptive will of God, the preferential will of God, and the discerned will of God. We went over how essential it is to know the will of God which is important for the strengthening of our faith. We cannot believe God will do something unless we first find out if He said He would do it.

In the third book, we went over two of the most important topics that any believer could learn about: forgiveness and provision. There are four petitions found in the middle section of this Model Prayer. In this book, we discovered the power of the first two:

Give us this day our daily bread: *A petition for provision.*

Forgive us our debts, our trespasses: *A petition for pardon.*

If there are two areas of life in which you will need the Lord's constant help, they are the areas of forgiveness and daily provision. None of us have it all figured out, and sooner or later, we are bound to make a mistake. God knew this, so He taught us specifically how to come to Him in prayer when we've messed up. We also discovered what God has to say about our money. Regardless of where we are at financially, we will always need God's help in this area, whether to meet our own needs or the needs of others. God has quite a bit to say on the subject of our finances. If you have been struggling in the area of giving or receiving God's forgiveness, or if you need a financial breakthrough, then I encourage you to go back and pick up the third book in this series.

If you have not read any of the previous books, it is essential reading that will bless you greatly. Now let's dive in to the last two petitions in our part of the sandwich structure:

- Lead us not into temptation: *A petition for guidance.*
- But deliver us from evil: *A petition for protection.*

Could you use a greater degree of God's protection and guidance? I know I can! Let's begin...

Lead Us

Lead Us

"LEAD US NOT INTO TEMPTATION" (Matthew 6:13 KJV). Now, this portion of the prayer forces us to consider a difficult question: Can a holy, righteous, undefiled, blameless, unblemished, virtuous God actually lead anyone into temptation? Before that question is answered, we need to establish what "lead us not into temptation" really means in the context of this text.

This phrase does not mean that God is the prime mover behind all temptations, nor does it mean that Christians can pray this prayer and automatically be delivered from all temptations. The answer to this dilemma is found in the fact that the word *temptation* has two meanings. First, it can mean "being tempted, with the goal of causing a person to sin." Or second, it can mean "a test or a trial to prove the validity of one's faith."

So, obviously, God never tempts anyone with the goal of causing them to sin, but He does test us. No one likes being tested, though, because times of testing mean times of acceptance or rejection. Once you're tested, you either pass or you fail. There is either promotion or stagnation, and you remain where you are. Hardly anyone looks forward to times of testing. Oftentimes, before you step into the next season of your life, you must pass a test. This can sound like God is a tough authoritarian who needs to qualify you for the position you are about to hold. But always keep in mind the one word that God uses to define Himself: *love*. His tests are not cruel, and they do not subject you to pain and torment. There is one author of destruction, and that is Satan. God has no evil in Him to subject you to a test through evil. So be careful never to blame an attack from the enemy as a test from the

Father. God does test us; Satan attacks and tempts us.

So, you need God's guidance to pass His test, but you also need His protection from Satan's attacks. Christ did not mention these two petitions in the same breath by accident. Even though these petitions are listed separately, they are also intertwined. They are linked. They are tied together. So, just as we need daily provision and daily pardon, we also need daily guidance and daily protection. After Jesus taught us to pray, "Give us this day our daily bread," He taught us to pray, "Forgive us our trespasses, as we forgive those who trespass against us." Then He taught us to pray, "Lead us not into temptation." And at the same time, He tells us to make a plea for God to deliver us from evil.

Let's look at the biblical evidence for God testing us:

Now it came to pass after these things that God tested Abraham.

—GENESIS 22:1

God did what? He *tested* Abraham; He did not tempt him. *"He tested Abraham, and said to him, 'Abraham!' And he said, 'Here I am.'"*

At appropriate times, God allows us to be put into situations where our faith is tested, and tried, with the ultimate goal of our faith being strengthened, and matured. That's the purpose. Trials and tests are the very soil in which the Christian believer grows. You will not grow as a Christian without trials or tests. So, you don't want to duck them; you don't want to skirt them. That's why it's important to have a very clear understanding of what Jesus meant when He said, "Pray this: Lead us not into temptation."

As Christians, we face two basic types of trials. The first are trials of correction, or trials of perfection. When God permits a time of testing or trial in the life of the believer, He's either trying to correct us to get us back on track so the devil cannot pluck us away, or He's trying to perfect us. He is never aiming to destroy us.

God chooses what we go through. We choose *how* we go through what we go through.

So, the clincher for going through a trial is our response.

Whatever we go through, these trials we are sent are to work for our good and for God's glory. As we journey through life, we can expect our faith to be tried and tested. The Christian life is filled with what I like to call "the ministry of trials, tests, and temptations." That is a ministry. Everybody is engaged, as Christian believers, in the ministry of trials, tests, and temptations. Not even Jesus was able to escape this ministry.

Don't be afraid of trials. Don't be scared of times of testing. Don't run away from temptation as a coward, because temptation, in and of itself, is not sin. It never becomes sin until you yield to it. Every test from God is not a temptation to sin; the failure to obey God becomes sin due to disobedience, but God does not test you with a vice to see if you are strong enough to withstand it. God never uses sin like Satan used the fruit of the Tree of the Knowledge of Good and Evil. When God tests His children, we should not be afraid because those trials are coming from His hand, and everything He does for us is because He loves us.

> *Every good gift and every perfect gift is from above, and comes down from the Father of lights, with whom there is no variation or shadow of turning.*

> —JAMES 1:17

Anything that comes from God is good. God doesn't have any bad in Him. It is Satan's practice to tempt you with sin, and then add condemnation after you give in to the temptation. God is the polar opposite of this approach. His tests are opportunities for blessings or reproof, based on our response to them. When you pass, you receive blessings, but even if you were to fail, God is right there to help you get back on your feet.

When Peter walked out on the water with Jesus, he soon failed his test of faith by noticing the wind and the waves, but Jesus did not let him sink. He reached out and helped Peter back to his feet, and then He reproofed him, asking, "Why did you doubt?" With those four words, Jesus was looking Peter in the eye, saying:

> *"Didn't you know that I was with you and wouldn't let anything happen to you? You were not out on the water alone. You were not facing the ferocious storm alone. The same waves barreling toward you were barreling toward Me, and if it was to overtake you, it'd have to overtake Me. Why did you not trust Me? Why did you doubt?"*

How often have we wrestled with God and failed our tests due to the same kind of doubt? Do not fear tests from your loving heavenly Father. How do you pass a test from your loving Father? You stay close to Him, you lean on Him for guidance, and come hell or high water, you hold on to Him and take Him at His word. Even if you fail a test, that's not the end—God doesn't write you off. If you fail the same test a thousand times, then God will pick you up a thousand times. God loves you—you must keep that in mind.

What does the Bible have to say about temptations and trials?

> *My brethren, count it all joy when you fall into various trials, knowing that the testing of your faith produces patience. But let patience have its perfect work, that you may be perfect and complete, lacking nothing.*
>
> —JAMES 1:2–4 NKJV

When you pray for more patience, you're actually praying for a lot of tests to come your way. But the goal, according to this Scripture, is to be "lacking nothing." That means that temptations, trials, and tests are supposed to add to your life at the end of the day! You should lack nothing after you pass the major tests. That's what the Scripture says. But you cannot expect God to bless you if you have no patience. Have you been saved for twenty years but you are still cussing out people when they make you mad? God can't trust you if you are like that.

The word *count* in those verses is written in the future tense. James was not saying that the *trial* is joy. He was saying that beyond the trial, there's joy. So, he's saying, "Count it all joy in the midst of your trials and testing. Think ahead. Look forward. Joy is coming if you stand."

When people have been cruel to you, when people have literally done evil to you and affected your life, your family, and your career, if you keep standing... then joy will be the result. When you lift weights in the natural, you willfully place stress on your body so it will grow stronger. Spiritually speaking, we know that the joy of the Lord is our strength! Similarly, in the natural, when we are under the stress of an adverse situation and our faith is being pressured and tested, even though we may feel tired and beaten up in the moment, we can keep standing and fighting because we know that we're going to grow stronger. We can count it all joy, and can press through the test because the blessings are worth it. The joy will come—believe that!

Let's read another passage along these lines:

> *Blessed is the man who endures temptation; for when he has been approved, he will receive the crown of life which the Lord has promised to those who love Him.*

> —JAMES 1:12

If you endure temptation, you are blessed. You are not blessed for experiencing temptation, you are not blessed for praying for temptation, you are not blessed for giving in to temptation—you are blessed when you *endure* it. How interesting it is that James doesn't say in this passage that you are blessed when you *overcome* temptation. Earlier in verse 2, James wrote that temptations work patience. Sometimes it is not a matter of rising above a situation, but rather gritting your teeth and outlasting it. Having done all to stand, you keep standing with your eye on the prize, namely, joy! You are blessed when you endure temptation. You are blessed! If you can hurdle a temptation, you are blessed in the sight of God, no matter how your flesh feels.

I'm not trying to suggest that this is easy. When people are being wicked and cruel and mean and nasty to you, it is not easy to stand there and not slap the daylights out of them! But oh, if you can endure it, God has blessings waiting for you. Even Job understood that—take a look at what he said:

"But He knows the way that I take; when He has tested me, I shall come forth as gold."

—JOB 23:10

You will come forth as gold! When the times of testing are over, it will be better for you if you stand.

> *Let no one say when he is tempted, "I am tempted by God"; for God cannot be tempted by evil, nor does He Himself tempt anyone.*
>
> —JAMES 1:13

God does not tempt anybody. So, you've got to have an understanding of what the phrase "lead us not into temptation" means. When you pray to God, "Lead us not into temptation," and God cannot tempt us, what does that mean?

The meaning of that text and the spirit behind this petition carries with it the same spirit as Jesus' prayer in Gethsemane, when He prayed, "My Father, if it's possible, let this cup pass from Me." That's the same spirit. This petition, "Lead us not into temptation," is a cry of emotion. It is a call from the heart of the believer. This petition is a safeguard against our own presumption and false sense of security. So when we pray, "Lead us not into temptation," we are praying something like this: "Father, spare us the trial, but if the trial is Your way and Your plan, then please protect us so that we may not only endure it, but we'll also grow from it."

When you pray this petition, you are not asking God to spare you from all the trials in life. You will not grow as a Christian if that's the case. This element of the prayer is more in agreement with 1 Corinthians 10:13:

> *No temptation has overtaken you except such as is common to man; but God is faithful, who will not allow you to be tempted beyond what you are able, but with the temptation will also make the way of escape, that you may be able to bear it.*

He will not allow you to be tempted beyond what you are able to bear. He didn't say He would stop the temptation, but God is so faithful that He will not allow you to be tempted beyond your ability to withstand it. This means that if you are a child of God, walking with Him, then whatever hell you are dealing with now, you can handle it. Like a boxer in the ring, you have an assurance that should put the biggest grin on your face—it's the assurance that whoever steps into that ring with you is somebody you can beat. You still have to fight the match—you still have to get bloody, beaten, and bruised fighting your opponent—but you can smile through the blood, sweat, and pain, knowing that if you won't surrender, then you will eventually win. The fight has been fixed, the headlines have already been written for tomorrow's newspapers, all you have to do is not give in or give up, and you will win! Even if the opponent who steps into the ring is a massive fellow, with muscles on his muscles, you should take one look at him and start rejoicing, because God just got done telling you that you have *big* faith! That big fella wouldn't be in the ring with you unless you could whip him! The bigger the opponent you face, the greater your praise should be! Like I mentioned earlier, the clincher is always your response to the situation. Will you dread the punishment and pain you are about to experience while fighting this opponent, or will you count it all joy and keep your eyes fixed on Christ, enduring to the last round? You just have to make sure you respond to the test correctly.

Some theologians have agreed that the word *lead* in this petition suggests "permission." So when we pray, "Lead us not into temptation," what we are praying is, "God, do not permit us or allow us to go down a path and enter into a trial that is too great for us, causing us to stumble and fall into sin." Don't permit us, not, "Don't carry us." This actually reflects the other elements in the prayer. Let's break this down a bit further.

God promises to meet the needs of the righteous according to His riches in glory by Christ Jesus. Yet we are to pray, "Give us this day our daily bread." God promises to forgive us of our sins, yet we still have to pray and petition for that forgiveness.

God promises that He will not allow us to get into a trial that is over our heads, but He will provide a way of escape also, that we may be able to endure it. Yet, we are to pray that He will not allow us or permit us to go into any trial that is beyond us.

Even though the Bible makes it very clear to us that God will provide, Jesus still told us to "ask." God promises to forgive our sins, and Jesus has already died for our sins, and yet He still tells us, "Ask God to forgive you every day." In the same way, God promises not to allow us to go beyond what we are able to handle and that He will always provide a way of escape. Yet He invites us to pray, "Lead us not into temptation…" So, God does not lead us into a life that is *free from trials and times of testing*. Rather, He teaches us that in the midst of them, we can look to Him for the necessary strength to deal with these trials and tribulations appropriately.

Now, here's what I want you to keep in your head: The growing, the nurturing, and the maturing of your faith always takes place in difficult times. Your faith never grows in calm waters. As long as everything is dandy and nice and smooth, your faith will not move. But it takes fire, it takes heat, it takes rejection, it takes lies, it takes scandals, it takes backstabbing, it takes a dry cupboard, it takes losing your job—it takes challenging times to grow your faith.

God does not lead us into a life that is free from trials and tribulations and tests. He sends these things. He allows these things. He permits these things in order to grow our faith, to nurture our faith, to mature our faith so that we become faith walkers. We should never be discouraged in times of trouble; we have access to God. If you have trouble, then God has trouble, and you can take your situation to the Lord in prayer. Can we find a friend so faithful as God? Who can handle our sorrows better than Christ? Who can undergird us in our weaknesses and not change His opinion about us other than Jesus? Who can lead us in the midst of tumultuous waters better than the Holy Ghost?!

Matthew 4:1 says:

Then was Jesus led up of the Spirit into the wilderness to be tempted of the devil.

Who led Jesus toward His time of temptation? The Holy Spirit. Jesus had to go through this in order to set the example for us, to lay the pattern down for us. This took place in Matthew 4. Jesus taught us the Model Prayer in Matthew 6. That trial, that time of testing with Jesus, could not come after the disciples asked, "Lord, teach us to pray." He went through a time of testing first. He went through a time of trial. And He was led into the wilderness by the Holy Spirit to be tempted by the devil, at a time when He'd just finished a forty-day fast. Please note that temptation is not punishment.

"Pray for me. I'm under heavy temptation."

There have been people in prayer lines who, when the minister gets to them and asks, *"How can I help you?"* respond something along these lines:

> *"I'm being tempted severely. Pray for my strength in the Lord."*

You've got to walk your way through to your strength. Nobody can pray that you be strengthened. Nobody can run that marathon, or lift those weights, or train their body for years, and then give you the benefits of their discipline. It doesn't work like that. If you want the strength, then you have to endure the tests, trials, and temptations to get the results. You have to resist the temptation to eat unhealthy food when the mouth-watering dessert is right in front of you. You have to endure under the intensity of the workout. You have to compete in trials and competitions to see where you are at compared to others and how far you still have to go. You need to get around others who are winning and see how you can be better.

We have made this way too complicated and willfully played the victim in our own lives. It's common sense that you can't eat a pizza and expect somebody else to get fat, or that you can reap the benefits of somebody else's workout routine, and yet when it comes to the exact same things, spiritually speaking, when you are going through various tests and trials, all of a sudden you accept the lie that it's complicated. It's not—you just have to endure it. You are not powerless! You have what it takes. I know this because God said He would not allow anything in your life to come along that you can't help but give in to it. In and of itself, temptation is not sin, but a feeling, an inclination, or a tendency that solicits us to go against the laws of God. But you do not have to give in! If you feel like you are collapsing under the stress, caving in under the pressure, don't you dare start speaking that out loud. You are a child of God, and in accordance with His Word, you can make it! You can cast your cares and worries on Him, you can find rest and peace in His arms, and you can pass the test!

I talk to people now and again, asking, "How are you doing?" And sometimes I wish I had never asked—Jesus, have mercy! They respond by unloading their burdens when all I was doing was being courteous. Now, don't get me wrong. I'm not advocating that as their bishop or friend, I roll my eyes and treat their situation with contempt. I genuinely love people, and I'll check my heart for what God would have me say to them in that moment to point them to Christ. However, if you are one of those people who is always carrying your burdens on your sleeves and then dropping them at the feet of anyone who asks, then you are about to lose all your friends and experience one defeat after another. You need to fight this thing with faith, and faith does not look to people to solve your problem for you; faith looks to God. That being said, if you need counsel, and if you are at the end of your rope, then it is wise to reach out to the elders of the church or your pastor and ask for help in regards to what Scriptures to stand on, or how to proceed in a biblical and godly manner. We are all together in this thing called life, and you ought not to feel condemnation when you are having a hard time hearing from God and the situation is getting worse. God loves you, and He wants to get help to you. But don't run to the elders the moment you experience a little pressure. And don't run to the church in the hopes that they will tell you something different than what God has already told you.

While it was the devil who tempted Jesus, it was the Holy Spirit who led Him into the wilderness, which means, then, that He had help. God does not need Satan, nor does He use Satan's temptations as tests, but oftentimes, in the middle of our tests, Satan can come to tempt us while we are emotionally, physically, or spiritually drained. It was the Holy Spirit who led Jesus into the wilderness, so Christ had a right to be in the wilderness, and He had the necessary authority to stand His ground. He had access to the Holy Spirit's strength and comfort to overcome both His test and His temptation. He was covered by the Holy Spirit! It was the same Holy Spirit who descended upon Him one chapter earlier, when He had just come out of His baptism, authenticating and validating that He was the Messiah. When you have the Holy Spirit with you, and you're submissive to the work and ministry and power of the Holy Spirit, the devil will never have victory in your life! During these times of testing, you've got to remember that God is not just the Alpha; He's also the Omega. He's not just the beginning; He's also the end. He's not just the first; He's also the last. That means that if He permitted it, He leads you out of it! God will not let the enemy triumph over you! What God has started, He will finish. People cannot stop it. Unexpected setbacks cannot stop it. Sickness cannot stop it. A temptation cannot stop it. Even your past failures can't stop it, because:

Being confident of this very thing, that He who has begun a good work in you will complete it until the day of Jesus Christ.

—PHILIPPIANS 1:6

God has started something in your life, and your trials, your tests, and your tribulations are coming into your life to strengthen you and to prepare you for where you're going—not to stop you from fulfilling God's plans for your life. You may need to take it a step further and speak aloud what Jesus said after being tempted by Satan three times in rapid succession.

Then saith Jesus unto him, Get thee hence, Satan: for it is written, Thou shalt worship the Lord thy God, and him only shalt thou serve.

—MATTHEW 4:10 KJV

Translation? Jesus said, "Enough!" Then said Jesus unto Satan, "Enough!" That's what you need to tell the enemy in your life: "*Enough!* I've had it! This is where it ends!" You are not saying it because you are at the end of your rope.

You are not letting all the emotional and mental stress boil up to the top and explode because of the pressure and pain you've been experiencing. No, this strong declaration was given by Christ after forty days of intense fasting and praying. He underwent an incredible amount of testing, built right into the human makeup. He gave up every form of food, entertainment, and even any and all of His social needs. And coming right at the heels of this test was a temptation from the enemy, trying to put his foot on Christ while He was vulnerable and expecting an easy score. Satan doesn't tempt you when you are at your best; most often, he will tempt you when you are at your worst: when you haven't prayed in days, or when you haven't fed on anything spiritually for weeks. He tempts you whenever you have had six other problems that day. However, Christ's response was not to put Satan out of His presence because of the desperation He might have felt. He put Satan out of His presence because He was tired of looking at him. Christ was sitting there, looking at him, thinking, "You could tempt Me all day and night, and I still won't succumb, so take a hike." And when He told Satan to beat it, there was faith behind it. We know this because of what happens in the next verse:

> *Then the devil leaveth him, and, behold, angels came and ministered unto him.*
>
> —MATTHEW 4:11 KJV

That's what Satan is trying to avoid. He'll do everything in his power to keep you focused on your own problems, meditating on how hard it is, how big your issues are, and how insurmountable your obstacles seem to be. He wants you to focus on how you feel, on how little you understand, and how weak you are. He knows that if any man, woman, or child were to read their Bible and step into their rightful place as a co-heir with Christ, a child of God, and an ambassador to the King, assuming the delegated authority bequeathed unto them by the

King, if they were to boldly stare down the enemy of their souls and declare, "You have no place in me, get lost!" then Satan has no choice. He must leave. Furthermore, it is in your best interest to gather yourself and rebuke the devil sooner rather than later, because the angels aren't coming to minister to you as long as you're still facilitating the devil. But when you say to the devil, "That's enough, this is where you jump off— if not, this is where I throw you off!" That's the angels' cue to jump in. So, temptations and trials and tribulations and evil are all a part of life, but there is a time limit attached to every trial, every time of testing. When you pray, "Lead us not into temptation," and you add the plea, "But deliver us from evil," then you are calling on God to be in remembrance of that time limit. You are saying, *"Lord, don't forget about me down here. I know You love me, and I know You'll take care of me, but I'm just reminding You that this evil down here is looking at me like*

I'm a tasty piece of meat, and I could use that deliverance any second."

Biblical scholars have suggested that both petitions could be translated accurately like this: "Save us during the time of trial and deliver us from the evil one." There's no part of your life that is untouched by evil. It has changed and oftentimes ruined circumstances, marred characters, and in many cases, it has even affected the whole of God's creation. The whole earth right now is groaning. In times like these we need to ask God every day to lead us not into temptation.

Deliver Us

Deliver Us

"DELIVER US FROM EVIL" IS THE FOURTH and final petition in category number two, which focuses on us.

1. The petition of provision: "Give us this day."

2. The petition of pardon: "Forgive us our trespasses."

3. The petition of guidance: "Lead us not into temptation."

4. **The petition of protection: "Deliver us from evil."**

This petition could be more accurately translated, "Deliver us from the evil one."

Evil, my friend, is real. There is no part of our lives that remains untouched by evil. In the general sense, evil is the opposite, or the absence, of good, although in everyday usage, "evil" often denotes profound wickedness. Both Testaments, the New and the Old, conclude that evil is the opposition to God, conducted by fallen angels that are led by a leader named Lucifer, or Satan.

So, this petition, "Deliver us from evil," is a needful and precious petition that Jesus taught His disciples and us to pray daily, because we are exposed to evil all the time—both visible and invisible evil. Somewhere, right now, people are calculating evil to come against you. You might know where they are in this world, where they are in this city, or which pew they're in, in your church. There's evil around us all the time. We are never far away from evil in this world.

So, Jesus said, "You ought to pray daily. Just like you pray for your daily bread and for your daily pardon, you ought to pray for your daily protection and deliverance."

The first thing we must understand is the admission Christ was making, and that we are now making, by praying the words, "Deliver us from evil." The first acknowledgment is this:

By praying, "Deliver us from evil," we are admitting that life is a struggle, that we are in warfare and are combatting an enemy who seeks to oppress, destroy, or negatively affect our relationship with our heavenly Father and keep us from fulfilling our life's purpose.

This is what the assignment of the enemy is. He's evil, and he has an evil assignment. He wants to mar your relationship with your heavenly Father so you can't pray properly, "Our Father, who art in heaven." Without a connection to the Father, we are easy prey. Satan is evil incarnate, based on the definition for evil mentioned earlier. He is in complete "opposition" to God. His evil assignment is to remove you from God, not because you are something special and he wants to take you out, but because you are something special to God and he wants to hurt God by hurting His kid.

In order to do that, he wants to make sure you don't see yourself as a child of God. And then, he wants to prevent you from fulfilling your purpose, not so you yourself will suffer personally, but so the kingdom will suffer.

We can become so egotistical when it comes to being attacked. However, the attack against you has got nothing to do with *you*. The devil is after what God can do *through you*. He's trying to stop you in order to further his evil goals. He will use evil things to divert you and move you away from your assignment.

The second acknowledgement is this:

When we pray, "Deliver us from the evil one," we are also acknowledging that there is not only evil in the world, but there is also a supremely evil one whose ultimate goal is to steal, kill, and destroy.

It is so important for us to realize these two facts. If problems and issues are not supposed to be in the life of a Christian, then all of us must be doing it wrong. We all have struggles that we face. We all live in a world with evil all around. However, what being a Christian does afford us is an answer to those questions and a solution to the problems that come up. We are not left defenseless; we are given the proper tools to be able to overcome. So, remaining ignorant or pretending there is not evil in the world, that there is not a supreme evil one in the world trying to devour us, will only leave us unprepared.

The second fact is that there is a supreme evil one, known as Satan, that wants to destroy you and kill your purpose! And he'll do it with evil intent. I implore you to be prayed up and sensitive to the Holy Spirit. You have to know how to smell evil, not just see it. You've got to sense it coming. This supremely evil one will always find at least one representative of his to place in your inner circle. Jesus was not left out of this process. Jesus chose Judas, just like you have chosen your friends—but some of them have been manipulated by the evil one.

See, Jesus chose Judas, and Judas became the representative of the supremely evil one, who sold Jesus out and betrayed Him. There's at least one person in your life who is not "for you," who wouldn't mind watching you fail. Now, I'm not trying to make you feel paranoid. Knowing there is evil all around and that it could come from a friend or family member does not mean you should just write them off. Even Peter yielded to the enemy at one point, yet Jesus did not write him off:

From that time forth began Jesus to shew unto his disciples, how that he must go unto Jerusalem, and suffer many things of the elders and chief priests and scribes, and be killed, and be raised again the third day. Then Peter took him, and began to rebuke him, saying, Be it far from thee, Lord: this shall not be unto thee. But he turned, and said unto Peter, Get thee behind me, Satan: thou art an offence unto me: for thou savourest not the things that be of God, but those that be of men.

—MATTHEW 16:21–23 KJV

Despite this stumble, Peter ended up doing incredible things for the Lord and for His people. We all have our "off days," so be careful not to treat your Peter like a Judas.

Sometimes the way the Lord delivers you from evil is by showing it to you. He might not come and remove the evil, but instead He reveals the evil to you and invites you to remove it yourself. He tells you to separate yourself from among them, so that you do not perish. You need to understand there is evil in this world. Sometimes good people will start out with you with good intentions, but then the devil gets ahold of them because he needs somebody in your inner circle. So instead of bringing in somebody, he chooses one whom you had already chosen and he corrupts them. Bad company corrupts good manners.

That's why you've got to keep praying in the churches.

There's evil in every level of our country, starting at the highest levels of government, down to the fraternity of law, the medical fraternity, and all other aspects of our society—including our churches. There's evil! Our country is becoming an evil-minded country. There are so many people in our country who do not have good intentions.

What has happened to us? We used to be our brother's keeper. We used to look out for one another. We were a tenderhearted, loving-minded, Christian country. But a little bit of money, a little bit of power, a little bit of success has totally corrupted and morally bankrupted our people! There's evil all around.

Are you tired of evil? Have you been hurt by someone close to you in the last few years? Have you been betrayed by a family member? Denied? Backstabbed? Maligned? Lied about? Scandalized? Evil has grown in the shadows, and we as a church have become oblivious to it. We now only think evil comes in the form of serial killers, child molesters, and rapists, when evil actually comes in all kinds of forms and is devoid of good intentions. So, why call out all the evil we experience in the world? Because of the last acknowledgment we make whenever we pray, "Deliver us from evil."

> *When we pray, "Deliver us from evil," we are acknowledging that even though God is sovereign, the evil one operates here in this earth realm, and we live and move and have our being behind the enemy lines.*

Don't let sophisticated, secularized people cause you to believe there is no Satan. Or that the evil one doesn't have the ability to cause issues here on earth. Evil is real in this world. Satan is real in this world, and he's on an assignment in this world to seek, to kill, and to destroy. In your flesh and of yourself, you are no match for him. But with Christ, it's a different story! That's why you have to sync up with Christ and pray every day, "Lord, deliver us from the evil one." When we do that, we are praying against everything that seeks to destroy us— all the wickedness of this world. When we pray, "Deliver us from evil," we are asking God to cause us not to be affected by the wickedness of this world. There is a supremely evil one who finds a way to use principalities, and powers, and rulers of darkness, and spiritual wickedness in high places, and other people, to wreak his havoc on the earth. But don't ever make the mistake of equating the power of Satan with the power of God. There's no comparison. There are no known units of measurement that could accurately show you the difference of power between the two. On the other hand, the devil doesn't like you. If you are a Christian, even though you're not perfect but you're striving to live for God, the devil can't tolerate you! But I have good news! Now that you know that there is evil in the world, and that it can come from anywhere except from Christ, then you can make your garrison in Him, your abode in Him, and He will set up shop inside of you. And who is it that can come against God and win?! The gates of hell shall not prevail against the church!

Now that we know evil exists, and that often Satan uses other people to get to us, how can we recognize evil to eliminate those relationships and protect ourselves and our loved ones? There are eight basic things that evil people do that are a dead giveaway of what is in their heart. No one can truly know another's heart, but the Bible says:

> *Beware of false prophets, who come to you in sheep's clothing, but inwardly they are ravenous wolves. You will know them by their fruits. Do men gather grapes from thornbushes or figs from thistles? Even so, every good tree bears good fruit, but a bad tree bears bad fruit. A good tree cannot bear bad fruit, nor can a bad tree bear good fruit. Every*

tree that does not bear good fruit is cut down and thrown into the fire. Therefore by their fruits you will know them.

—MATTHEW 7:15–20

You can know the caliber of a person based on their actions. So many people cry out against others, saying things like, "You don't know my heart," and "You're just judging me." You don't need to condemn people, or go out of your way to tell people they are evil, but when you cut off a relationship because they are into evil things, don't let them accuse you of being judgmental. You need to judge them worthy or unworthy of holding a position in your life so you can protect yourself and your loved ones. You may not know their hearts, nor their intentions, but you can see their fruit, and if you don't want to eat that fruit, then stay away from it! So, how can you tell the difference between the good and the bad fruit?

How can you recognize when people are evil? First of all, from my research, evil people don't just practice evil ignorantly. They know they're evil, and **they have no immediate plans or intention of changing. They're evil. They enjoy being evil. And they look for rewards as a result of their evil doings.** There are wicked and evil people in this world, and unless you have a strong spirit of discernment, you'll never know they are evil until after they strike.

So, evil people sometimes are referred to as "depraved," "wicked," or "sick" people. They will come from a place you least expect. They could come from your school: wicked schoolteachers teaching evil doctrine and engaging in illicit behavior behind closed doors. They could crop up at home or when you are out with friends. Although you may be feeding on the right things, whenever you get around your friends and family, you start partaking from what they have been feeding on. These people could show up on your job, performing every sort of evil deed from selfish motives. You can even find them in your place of worship! There's wicked all around you. Don't be naïve in believing you are the most righteous person, who will not be touched by any evil. You're ignorant if you think that is true.

Now, first, *evil people enjoy watching other people in pain.* If you're around those who enjoy seeing people in pain— who have no compassion, no sympathy, no empathy—they're evil. Evil people are often victims of the prisons they've built for themselves. The problem is that watching other people's pain dulls their own pain. My friend, you've got to get to the place where you keep your eyes open for people who turn your worries and your pain into a joke. If you are in pain and they're making a joke out of it, they're evil!

Second, **evil people need to always be in control.** They often feel uncomfortable and powerless if they're not in control of every area of their lives. They don't trust anybody with any aspect of their lives.

And if you are not careful, they'll fool you because they can come off as being so polite, meticulous, punctual, and efficient, but in the back of their minds, they're waiting to strike. When you let them closer, deeper into your life, because you notice how polite they are and how mannerly they are and how efficient they are, soon you will discover, before you know it, they're now controlling your entire life. So, we've got to pray every day, "Lord, deliver us from evil."

The third sign of an evil person is that **whenever an evil person has been in your presence, they often leave you feeling drained and physically exhausted.** Oftentimes the surest sign that someone is evil is that you just don't feel right around them. You get creepy feelings, but you can't put your finger on what it is about them. You spend your time and energy trying to figure out what it is about this person. What is it? Something isn't clicking, and you don't feel right with that person. Evil can pretend to be good, but those persons carry their evil spirits with them. And if you are spiritual, you will sense it—behind their laugh and their smile, you can sense evil.

Fourth, **evil people laugh at the misfortune of others.** They trip out over bad news. Bad news gets them excited. When there's bad news on the television or the internet, they pull out their popcorn. There is a joyful reaction to other people's misfortune. They lack compassion. And every day we ought to pray... "Lord, deliver us from evil."

There's something sick and twisted about a person who will fall into this next category. Fifth, **evil people think it's funny when they insult you.** They insult you with no remorse. They insult you and laugh at you. They want everybody else to laugh too. It's a big joke to call you fat! They look at you and say, "Boy, she has a..." whatever it is that hurts your feelings. And then they laugh and want everybody else to laugh at it too. It's evil to degrade God's creation. It's evil.

Sixth, **evil people are very deceptive.** They're just as capable of showing kindness as anyone else, but there's a price that comes along with their kindness. They are great deceivers. Oftentimes evil people will be kind to you only to get something they think they need from you. For some, it's money. For others, it's sex. And for others, it's subservience. They'll be kind to you until they strip you. Manipulating people is the order of the day for them. They know how to get people to do whatever they want them to do. It's manipulation. And who they affect in the process is of no issue to them.

Seventh, **they major in belittlement.** They spend time belittling people. It comes in a lot of different forms. It comes so often that evil people look at other people and all they see are toys—people become items to be played with. It's evil to take the lives of other people and make games out of them. Some people are struggling, not only trying to make it, but struggling with their own identity, struggling with their sexuality, struggling with their past, struggling

with their future, and you belittle them.
They may spend a lot of time ridicul-
ing your appearance. I don't like this. I
don't like this about you. I don't like red
on you. I don't like blue on you. I don't
like orange on you. The orange makes
you look broad. They ridicule your
body. You need to do this. You need to
do that. How do they get there? They're
evil people.

They go after your interests, your
hopes, your hobbies, your goals, your
friends, your house, your dreams—
anything is a target of belittlement for
these people.

Finally, eighth, **they despise people
who are more successful than them.** They
can't stand the fact that they are not the
smartest or the most successful in the
room. They are obsessed by their own
success. They'll go to great lengths in
order to prevent other people from being
successful, progressive, or productive.

**So, now that we recognize the evil,
and we do our part to eliminate it from
our lives as best we can, then what?**

When Jesus included this petition in the Model Prayer, He was not only encouraging us to pray, but He was also registering His divine opposition to evil. He was pointing to our heavenly Father as the only Source of deliverance from evil. When it comes to evil, you don't go to evil people to deliver you from evil. So, if you're already catching hell, you think that evil people can help you out of your own evil? First of all, when you're covered in the blood of Jesus, nobody can "fix" you. If your heart is fixed and your mind is already made up that God is your Deliverer, then you are not looking for other people to fix you or put your life back together. You are looking to God, and God can use other people to help accomplish this. There are godly men and women who can add to your life just like there are evil people who will take away from your life. We can't control the good or the evil people though, so as far as it depends on us, we are looking to God for help and judging people's fruit to see if they are from God or from the devil.

Now, Jesus had something very interesting to pray, coming down to the end of His journey. He's about to be crucified, and He's giving His last report in the form of a prayer:

> *"I do not pray that You should take them out of the world, but that You should keep them from the evil one."*

> —JOHN 17:15

In one part of the prayer, He said, "Lord, I pray, Father, that You don't take these disciples out of the world, but that You keep them from the evil one." This is really the *Lord's* Prayer.

Jesus said, "I pray, Father, that You keep these—these people whom I've called, and these whom I've had surrounding Me for these last three years as I get ready to complete My assignment and go on to My celestial journey. Keep them away from the evil one." Why did He pray that the Father not take the disciples out of the world, though? Because they still had a job to do! Christ didn't want them to just be safe from the evil one—He wants them to play a role in the evil one's demise. He wants His disciples to learn faith, to learn how to flow with God and to call Him "Father," just as Christ did. He wants them to be more than conquerors, and not to just be saved from any evil by God taking them to heaven. He wanted the disciples to be part of bringing heaven down to earth. And they did just that on the day of Pentecost!

Lastly, when we pray, "Lead us not into temptation, but deliver us from evil," like Christ in the Garden of Gethsemane, we are praying, "Lord, permit us not to enter into any form of temptation that we cannot handle, but deliver us from the evil one."

Most people in this world, at some point in their lives, discover that they're in bondage to something or someone. There's a deep longing in most of us to be free from that which binds us. One thing we know for sure is that God, our heavenly Father, is the great Deliverer. Our perplexity cannot baffle His wisdom. Our needs cannot exhaust His resources. And our sorrow cannot distance His sympathy. He's a great Deliverer. Psalm 91:14–15 helps us to settle this in our hearts:

Because he has set his love upon Me, therefore I will deliver him; I will set him on high, because he has known My name. He shall call upon Me, and I will answer him; I will be with him in trouble; I will deliver him and honor him.

When you declare your love for the Lord, and when it is clear to God that you love Him with all your heart, with all your mind, and with all your soul, in the day of trouble, according to the Scriptures, God will not only deliver you, but He'll set you in a place of honor.

The body of Christ is made up of "ex" everything: ex-sinners, ex-haters, etc. Everything you could possibly think of, one of the members in the body could stand up and say, "That was me." From rapists to murderers to drug addicts to hustlers and pimps and punks and prostitutes, lesbians to thieves, all kinds of "exes" make up the body of Christ. But let me tell you something, when God delivers you from your "ex," then your "ex" doesn't count anymore! He is the great Deliverer! Amen!

Once God has delivered you, don't let other people throw your past in your face. And if they do, acknowledge it and say, *"Yes, that's what I used to be, but now God has given me the opportunity to see life from a different perspective. I was sinking deep in sin, far from the peaceful shore. I was very deeply stained within, sinking to rise no more. But the Master of the seas, heard my dispelling cry. And from the waters, He lifted me; now safe am I! Love lifted me! **And... love can lift you, too, if you'll let Him**"*

Jesus admonishes us that when we pray, we ought to say, "Lord, deliver us from evil."

LEAD US & DELIVER US

If you need deliverance from sin, pray this prayer:

Lord, deliver us from the evil one!

If you need deliverance from affliction, pray this prayer:

Lord, deliver us from the evil one!

If you need deliverance from any wickedness perpetrated against you, pray this prayer:

Lord, deliver us from the evil one!

If you need deliverance from sickness and disease, pray this prayer:

Lord, deliver us from the evil one!

God has the power and the desire to deliver you. The Lord shall preserve you from all evil. The Lord shall preserve your soul. He shall preserve your "going out" and your "coming in" from this time forth. When the wicked, even your enemies, come up against you, they will stumble and fall. Although a host shall encamp against you, your heart shall not fear. Fret not yourself because of evildo-ers, neither be envious of the wicked, for they shall soon be cut down. Trust in the Lord and do good. Delight yourself in the Lord, and He shall give you the desires of your heart. He is a Deliverer!

About The Author

Bishop Neil C. Ellis is the presiding prelate of the Global United Fellowship (GUF), with more than 1,400 churches in 42 countries. GUF serves as an international body of spiritual leaders, fellowships, and congregations united to strategically plan, implement, and execute transformative and generational change.

Bishop Ellis is the senior pastor of Mount Tabor Church in Nassau, Bahamas. This church has grown from 11 charter members in 1987 to thousands of members and thousands more who are a part of the Internet Church, Mount Tabor Anytime. As a pastor to pastors, he mentors a large number of pastors around The Bahamas, Europe, and the United States and serves as a counselor and advisor to hundreds of pastors around the world.

Bishop Ellis has been recognized by Her Majesty, Queen Elizabeth of England, for rendering distinguished services in Commonwealth nations and is also the recipient of the 2010 Trumpet Award for Spiritual Enlightenment. He is the youngest living inductee in the International Civil Rights Walk of Fame located in Atlanta, Georgia. He is also the author of several books and is a much sought after conference speaker and prophetic teacher.

Bishop Ellis and his wife reside in Nassau, Bahamas along with their two children.